TEMPERAMENTS

Poems by David Dragone

DAVID DRAGONE

"For Joanna"

Table of Contents

Acknowledgments.............................vii

It Has To Mean Something.......................1

The Secret Spot..............................2

Early Snowfall in The Woods....................4

Sara......................................5

Errant Turn.................................6

Half Luddite................................8

By Purgatory Chasm.........................10

Upon Awakening 11

The Blizzard...............................12

Winter Scene 14

Short Dance of The Gulls.....................15

Moon Sonata 16

Waterfire.................................17

Archer 18

The Skipping Stone 19

Birdsong 20

Mommy, What was War Like? 22

Fourth of July Fireworks 24

Just Another Piano Tuning 26

Ambition.................................28

Late Winter Thaw 29

Migration Song 30

Sea-Glass.................................31

Breakdown Lane 33

Windy Maples on The Cliff-Walk 35
Interrupted Commute 36
The Fishing Trip 37
Divorce Record - 1970 39
Lethal Injection 41
Mr. Gallo at Eighty-Seven 42
On A Day Like This 44
Beacon 46
Spring Decision 47

ACKNOWLEDGMENTS

I would like to thank the following publications:

Avocet:
The Secret Spot, Early Snowfall In The Country, Moon Sonata, Sara, Errant Turn, Spring Decision, Winter Scene

Common Ground Review:
Half Luddite, Archer, Beacon

Bryant Literary Review:
The Fishing Trip, Lethal Injection

California Quarterly:
Short Dance Of The Gulls, Late Winter Thaw

Providence Sunday Journal Poetic License Column:
Waterfire, Mr. Gallo At Eighty-Seven

Rhode Island Public Radio:
Mr. Gallo At Eighty-Seven, Waterfire

Trinity Repertory Company:
Mr. Gallo At Eighty-Seven

Newport Life Magazine:
Blizzard, By Purgatory Chasm, Upon Awakening

IT HAS TO MEAN SOMETHING

Life is short
But it's the longest thing I'll ever do
So it has to mean something.
My time remaining shortens
And I get up earlier than I used to.
I'm squeezing more time into time.

I hear the birds sing at sunset too
Wondering where they'll nest their voices
After nightfall.
Life is short
But it's the longest thing I'll ever do
So it has to mean something.

My dreamy ear listens
To the notes it missed in its day-song
As I reel under predawn light.
I watch early birds
Fishing their lamped ocean
Hooked on hope, and I've joined them

Because life is short
But it's the longest thing I'll ever do
So it has to mean something.

THE SECRET SPOT

When you stop looking
Your secret spot reveals itself —
Someplace you could stay forever.
Trees die, leaving armfuls of legacies
Collected to fuel us.
Dead limbs clutched against ribs —
We lay them out inside our hearths,
We fire dreams, we warm us close.

My son, green wood lives
To bend over backwoods,
But unseasoned, can't comfort you.
Only dead wood breaks with proud snaps
When you take it against your knee
And pull hard. My son,
You must find some wood
With enough soul left for music.

Music doesn't need to change the world
When it helps us bear the imperfect.
Wind plays rustle songs using tree voices
Swaying around tunes deep in our forests.
The draw of horsehair across violin strings
Sings and dances life into seasoned wood
Even when wrong notes sometimes sound.
And fire burns loudest when licking its wounds.

Practice playing as hard as you can.
Season after season, look for wood
As thin as a string to start kindling
As thick as your fingers, igniting branches
As big as your arms. Gather enough wood
For whatever fire you need
Somewhere. Build it with found treasure,
Listening to where music comes from.

EARLY SNOWFALL IN THE WOODS

A muffling white confetti
Against the unlit sky
The country snow falls
Unspoiled
As if some tired stars are falling
To join me in my rest.
Many are on my face
As I get up to stretch
The limbs of trees
Too blanketed with snow
To join me.
It does not matter.
The trees
Welcome the quiet quilt
Of sleep.
I must stay awake
To enjoy this wintry nest.

SARA

Years ago, you were big enough to walk
But not run, and the kitchen sink was magic.
We took out the dishes and old glasses
Forks, knives, and everything else
And cleared the way for your bath.
It was like an altar.

And it was wonderful enough
So that twenty years later
When I found two old pieces of notepaper
With a few lines of stuff I'd written about it
I cheered and ran around the house
Waving my winning lottery tickets.

So this became a poem that grew somewhere
Between the cloudy ribs of light the moon pried open
Behind the joyous hospital that night
Years ago, when you were waiting to be born.

And later on, when you learned to ride your bike
At the abandoned tennis courts
You told me that if I let go too soon
You would kill me.
You looked at me a lot
With wobbly glances over your unsure shoulder.

I kept telling you to keep the wheel straight
And keep on pedaling
Long after you'd already learned how.

ERRANT TURN

Evergreens evade the naked hours
Never surrendering emotion's colors.
Woodenly planting green smiles
Passion's shortened hour
Watches oaks, clenched against loss.

Somewhere inside, evergreen rings brown
From risking nothing, marking time
Knowing nothing about gold and blush.
Men learn about oaks early
About all things risked without surrender
Holding colors close in their fists.

Maybe when your car hits a squirrel
Launching its broken body end over end
Right in front of the windshield, time stops
Your teenage son's quivering lip
With struggled swallows
Trapped in his cage of pain.

More clenching, tears unable to fall
Like ripe leaves.
When colored tears rake silent cheeks
Icy trees shine and snow spills magnificent
Against the sun. Unable to thaw
What other men have frozen

Scars live at the root of something
Left for dead —
Hues held close far too long.
Oaks don't give up anything easily —
Wind sways and batters them
Until they season enough
To shake it off like men.

HALF LUDDITE

I'm not a Luddite
But I wrote this on an Olivetti Underwood.
That's a typewriter. You can Google it.
When I was done, the fresh cotton paper
Gently unrolled in clicks as I slowly pulled it out
Twisting the knob and checking the ribbon
To see if I'd gotten things twisted up or shredded
From overuse. Too many words could do that.
I was careful about mistakes
Because I didn't want to rip paper or be typecast
As an eraser. That would just muddy things up.
I already had that problem.
I didn't like having to line the paper up again
To etch better ink
Into the first wrong impression I'd made,
Even though you can't see it here.
You'd be able to see the changing pressures
Of imprints into the paper
And where I'd gone a little deeper
Into the cotton marrow — subtleties
You just won't feel when you read this version
Because I was kidding you.
I don't have my Olivetti anymore.
This was printed on my Brother printer,
And cotton and linen paper are passé.
I tossed my Olivetti.

It just couldn't write very well
But it spoke loudly
When it got a second life as dumpster decoration.
That's all I have to say about it.
But I want some meat
On the bones of my instrument again.
I want to listen to something clack
Around its skeleton keys —
Letters on the ends of each steely arm
Leaving creased paper skin tattooed with ink
As my fingers push each chrome-ringed key
And shrug the typewriter carriage up to the page
For another letter. I heard every typewriter
Has its own fingerprint — little quirks
In the way a particular letter
Might have been forged with a nick.
Anyhow, it looked like a cash register.
I never make any money with it, though.
That's another reason I had to put it down.
I want it back. Long before the Olivetti
Guys with quill pens put different finger pressures
Into nuanced words
With stress points of the feathered wing.
Letters flew across diplomatic lines
Over tightropes — too many wrong words
Could topple the world. But even before that
You could pass secret messages
With invisible ink if you were good enough.
Now, everything seems always never new.

BY PURGATORY CHASM

The woods held love-carved trees
Names chiseled out of branching limbs
Forested moments etched with forever intent
On their sturdy oaken bones.
Time found its way around every violator's cut
And smoothed its road over gnarled bark
Where green grew from scab to woody scar.

The sea's passion clobbered rocks
And launched itself so high
That it hung almost weightless and forever,
As if poised to stop misty time
Before it fell back into pockmarked stone
To unweave its briny blood.

Seasons grew hugs around names
That still lived under the skin
And the sea kept rubbing salt
In its own shore of complaint
Turning things over and over
While you stayed perched
On some smooth rock
That had no name.

UPON AWAKENING

It will be about how trees
Will realize they're terminal
But not knowing when
Will decide their fall blooms
Can no longer be wasted
Trying to impress the sky.

It will be about how they'll shed their suits
Of loud armor, giving up gold victories
Their banners dwindling
And wounded in the fray of lancing wind.
Shrugging off autumn's robe
They will unclothe dreams

Spilling rainbows at their feet
And frost will help them let go.
It will be about how clouds lid the moon
As night skies clamp shut their mouths
Darkly clenching stars
With hope grinding their teeth,
And about how the world will turn in its tossings
Until dawn steels itself again.

It will be about how wintry suns
Shift their shine, becoming weathered
With too many seasons of runaway light
Straggler leaves flash-dancing between breezy stages
Hoping for warm notice
As they finally leave the tree
And go back to where they came from.

THE BLIZZARD

During the blizzard
I lost power for 24 hours.
I lit by hurricane lamp.
I hauled in snow-caked wood
And warmed the room with it.
It was fun until the next morning
When the house got cold.
It had dropped to fifty degrees
And my breath fogged.
I rolled out of bed
And my toes found the rude
Unwelcoming floor.
I lit a fire but it didn't do much good.
I set the faucets on slow drip
Just to keep things flowing
And put an old grate over the fire
To make hot soup and chili.

I felt like a pioneer.

Someone told me folks used bed-warmers once
Before they'd tuck themselves in
On cold winter nights.
Now I knew why. It was fun
To watch the world get so wild
That no one could stop it.
Snow bands whipped by—

Windows bowed and boiler flue-pipes
Moaned in cold tones
With every gusty warning.
It sounded brutal.
I wondered if anyone was out in it.
There was a hand-crank radio
That could have told me what was going on
But I could see and hear enough,
So I turned it off
And wondered how long
The battery would last.

When some nameless heroes
Got the power back on
Everything hummed back to routine
And streets full of tired plowmen
Kept going the next morning
Heaving white arcs into mountains
And my car was buried, so I made soup.

WINTER SCENE

Winter winds moved lean branches
Into cold clacks above backstreets
After ice storms left frozen sheaths
Around their glassy stems.
Gusts broke branches
And they fell and shattered —
Sunlight angled into rainbands
Arcing the fallen blush of oak leaves
That clung to fall as long as they could

Before shivering through their chilling fall.
Breeze raked the empty trees
Clicking bone songs in their limbs
And you watched it all, and you watched too
After you walked to the shore
As wind shaved wave tops into misty trimmings
Where slivered moonlight coined silver.
You saw how sunset seas could be on fire
And how the trees, branch to branch
Nerve to brittle nerve
Took the cold night-wind
Long stripped of fall's leafy whispers
And made its own language
As winter rubbed its skin
Over brittle tree bones
Coldly clinking crystal.

SHORT DANCE OF THE GULLS

They soared and swung in the stained sky
And went beyond the red-hearted.
They consumed the horizon's
Every studied morsel and fed themselves careless
Which kept them dancing
Around their split, crusty divisions.
Their loud screeching drowned the angry sea
And accused its tossing of being nothing more
Than high tide's salty screed.
They stabbed their gull-beaks into shells
And pried them open like a promise, as if
Their very survival depended on it
And then flew off towards sunset
Galloping across the unbridled sky
Saddled to the wind.

MOON SONATA

Yesterday's moony lovers
Imagined spun light in their hair
And took shadow-play's measure of naked light
Under tree branches that danced
Beyond the leash of their breezy reach.
Whispers rustled in their hands
As they passed secrets limb to limb
In laughter's passioned silhouette.

Bark sparkled black and white
Under widened eyes, the moon
Lit birches, their stirred leaves
Lashed darkly through forms
Half trammeled under a crescent moon
That clutched its remains — edgy with dark
Dry seas. Two trees exchanged touch
And swayed over wood-paths
That stood every walk of love
And kept on moving everything.

They continued their dance
And swayed ring by ring
Over some breathy new love that
Waited to find light recaptured
From the same old moon.

WATERFIRE

It started when drums raised bumps
On our animal skins and quickened every pulse
That dipped into water's long baptism —
The evolutionary font of skies.
Embers crawled down each wick with flashpoints
That waited over the city's heart, and fire
Was a magic that drums could bring back
From any darkened world that eclipsed us.
The twilight gondolier stroked nearly soundless
Winks into our canals — no certain journey
Gave itself to each oar-twist that kissed crisp air
Between slices of water that had to wrinkle
With the trip. He steered by the tilt of himself
In chosen directions, buoyed by his skill
Until the carriage of his pride
Became the pride of his carriage.

The hypnotic Indian danced as he whirled fireballs
That roused the limbic in us — crackle-flung
Sparks burned like stars in the pitch
Until they lived framed in cell phone photo
Constellations that painted our eyes before they
Flickered out — and the white-robed mime
Frozen in time
Waited to blow us a kiss for a buck.
We outlived every star we made
In our kindled image that night.
We kept glowing long after giddy throngs
Emptied both sides of a street between water, fire
And wakes that waved by every boat-keeper.

ARCHER

Into the wind
With studied aim
The equation of pitch and yaw
Is held drawn, triangulated
Against the grain of an elbow.

Knotted fingers unfurl release
From the straining line's rippling harness
As arrow seeks target
Feathering puffs of air aside
With tilted balance.

At the origin, critical moments pass.
Remaining range is mirrored
In the archer's eye
Creased with impatience
Inwardly concentric
And diminishing.

THE SKIPPING STONE

My un-grown daughter is as tall as my wife.
She is ripening for someone
My smile will someday admit
Into the house she'll be leaving.
In the deepest dark
There are points of music
Making love to the sky.

We look at the starry past — unbelieving.
She found you the perfect skipping stone
Dancing at the edge of the sea,
Before the sea could swallow it.
Can a stone be older than stars?
It always comes to this — our hearts
As thirsty as the fallen leaves
We grew. Everyone needs
To be someone's everything.

When she marries, breaking away
For the last time, the weight of it
Will be in my hand. I'll skip the stone
Over the ocean as she waves.

BIRDSONG

They can burst into the same song
That notes their dawn each morning
And can still sound it new in them.

They can go to the furthest edge
Of the windy lit limb and dance on
Hearts able to soar even in rain.

They stay unruffled about falling
Or becoming ungrounded between flights
Song tunes living under their wings

Flapping away in measured tempo
Attuned to every tilt and swoop, as if
They don't even have to work for it

Some lightness in their bones
Going beyond the beyond
Brushing sky with instinct

Living elsewhere in their otherness
Immersed in promise, each day
Aiming without aiming, without searching

For what's already gifted
And not having to worry about what storms come
As they fly, tinging magic into the sky

From dawn to dusk
Grateful for each new day
Like this one.

MOMMY, WHAT WAS WAR LIKE?

The sun was terrified to rise
Over another dawning horror
Where rubbled streets
Were already filled
With too much mourning.
Battles kept beating the living daylights
Out of moonshine
As explosions rattled the thunderstruck
Before erasing their lives.
Every soldier's red-inked war book
Cracked its burdened spine
At the heavy violence that opened
Each new chapter.

People wearied of news and sound bites
That squinted hearts, while high-noon shadows
Swallowed themselves as they tried in vain
To bandage hate's unshaded glare.

The smoke that filled their lungs
Burned from no peace pipe
As lightning stormed the innocent
With bombs raining down.

At night, survivors bolted every door
Rifling through fears
As they loaded hope's chambers.
They looked at the injured moon
And saw how its crescent
Had become some un-heavenly blade
That could cradle no star
As the better trains of civil discourse derailed
And the broken ribs of clouds bled somber colors
Into dusk, and the evening news
Kept coldly adding up the numbers
Of the subtracted.

FOURTH OF JULY FIREWORKS

From behind the grove of trees
Men with flares diffuse a bleed
Into the night's misted air.
Crimson rain falls illumined
From sparking limbs as they touch
Fuse to fuse with unflagging vigil.

Fire rises up to a sky beyond this earth, our earth
As we watch men launch rockets.
They claim themselves ascendant
To the spectacle we make of towed heads
And each climbing dream's intent
To flash in the whites of targeted eyes.

Explosions of color umbrella air
Over the grounded crowd — smoky husks
Drifting off in aftermath.
Kindled promise weeps down like a willow
Never touching, almost
Never to touch again

The same soil they rose from.
Shadows don't dance silent here in this world —
Round punctuating charges of darkness

Slam concussions into lungs
Stealing the breath of candles.
Flags are waving — for a long time
Will wave the colors
Of blood, bone, and sky.
They fray in the wind

Where we watch fireworks bloom
In the dark fields at nightfall.

JUST ANOTHER PIANO TUNING

There was nothing unusual about it.
I was let into the house by appointment.
I slung my tool-pack off and put it down
All top heavy and slouching against the wall.
Her piano was fairly new
And the casework was almost unblemished.
She was about eighty, but seemed very sharp
As she watched me. I pushed the red felt
Muting strip between strings
And checked pitch.

I tuned as she listened and paid bills at her kitchen
Table around the corner. We each did our jobs
Until I reached the tenor section. She came out
And took a break. I stopped working too.
She watched as I rolled up the first felt strip
Into cozy circles.

Then she told me the piano had been a gift
From her husband. She told me
They'd been married fifty-three years.
She told me he'd been a good man and a good father
And that he liked to listen to her play.
He'd been sitting on the couch
When the family found him
After returning from errands.
She showed me exactly where he'd been sitting.
She said he probably didn't have any pain.
It had been awhile, but people still asked her
If things had gotten any easier since then.

She had her piano playing for the senior center
And her children and grandchildren.
She had her chorus of friends.
She told me it was the routines and the little things
She missed most, and that she remembered
More of them each day.

She told me
About how they used to get settled in together
For the night
While she'd get his favorite snack ready
And he did Sudoku puzzles.
She told me
How they used to like watching *Jeopardy* together.
I stood there with my tuning hammer, listening.
She said fifty-three years was a good long time.

AMBITION

It wasn't what I thought.
Ambition's rutted road got worn
Breaking my carriage wheels
Like how my patience became old
Before I lost it
Pointing my blame finger
At the careless sky.

Summer sun spilled gold
As every step treasured my hunted thirst
Under high noon's glare.
Parched and saddled with burdens
My tired heart was an old horse
Whipped into pounding
By hope's hungered jockey.

I grazed in empty fields
Looking for full-course meals
On plates heaped with praise and roses.
I kept on complaining
About not getting my just desserts
Until I almost starved
From tabling gratefulness.

LATE WINTER THAW

Yesterday
The sun kissed
Snow-covered hills
And they shone and shrugged
Their cold shoulders
Against the scattered thaw.
Seagulls
Brushed their ink-tipped wings
Across the sky's limitless hug
Which loved the world warm.
They painted the sky with dizzy ease
And floated with clouds
That swabbed their ground's passion
Until joy swept up and wept
To recycle itself, and
The arms of trees
Stretched in soaky wonder
The next morning
When the world answered in rivers
I love you.

MIGRATION SONG

Paint the sky eggshell windswept white.
You tell me there's no such thing
Without even a passing glance at southward geese
Flapping away from cold and scolding northern.

They fly at their horizon, land scrabbling at your feet
For meals you give them stale.
Migration's imperatives green
With each flown mile's magnetic season

Goosenecks stretching like wind socks
In the crisping breeze.
Gulls beat scars into the wind
To reclaim their spot. Dusk slides in

And soothes the scalded sky.
Feathered wing tips rake dizzy air
Swooned and tipsy as they fly
To wherever they can hatch
And nest in southern's warmth.

SEA-GLASS

Half submerged
My palm frisked around sea glass —
Broken bottle parts inviting timid fingers.
I scoured buried treasure, my heart-sized fist
Opened to feel around sharp risk.
My seabed furrowed around glinting hints
But before I could get a good grip
A wave came in, slapped me hard
And rode my shore with erosion's whip.

For years, I lost many chances —
My boat too timid after rafts of scrapes.
I trolled moon-sifted shadows under silent skies
And lamped tight-lipped tides.
Where were my tools to harvest seaweed?
My rudder raked reefs —
Kissed murky shorelines under midnight's cuttings
And yielded to sunrise but found nothing
But un-shelled, drifted whisper-language.

The planks of aged shipwrecks stayed submerged
But still decorated beached hopes.
The sea raged as the world awakened, fogs hoisted
But still partly hung over yesterday's harbored
Failures. Unfinished sea glass flashed
While morning light pried open clouds
Unbolted beams, and flared jacked-up heaven
Amid the aimless gulls.

Clouds tried to stanch bleeds of early morning
Crimson, as my half-slumbered ocean
Lapped against some carefree dawn.
I tried to swagger fearless, looking for swag.
I chased ripened sunrise
Overshadowed by my silhouette
Until I found some gems whose hard edges
Had resigned to the simple things
That were already beautiful
And that was the rub.

BREAKDOWN LANE

After breaking down, he looked under the hood
And figured it must be the carburetor.
There was plenty of gas but the knocking betrayed
Him. Maybe impurities were moving through the fuel
Line — maybe the spark plug contacts were dirty —
Maybe he had no clue. He was a guy's guy though,
So even when he wasn't sure why
The car wouldn't kick over, he'd try something else
Framing every false start with a knowing picture
On his face.

His girlfriend made a suggestion
Of what might be wrong.
He said something back to her
But only in his mind. He shook his head
With a frowned eyebrow
Feigning a growing awareness.
He wasn't going to ask for directions.
He was listening to the struggling motor
Unable to admit he was rattled.
He was secretly glad when he spied his girlfriend
Furtively dialing triple A.
He started memorizing a raft of things
That might be wrong. He wanted to make sure he
Could tell the tow truck driver what he figured it
Could be.

He stayed outside the car
Striking his best hunter-gatherer pose
With the hood still up.

When the tow truck pulled in and the driver got out,
Her long hair and knowing grin
Silenced his engine
And his defenses broke down.

WINDY MAPLES ON THE CLIFF-WALK

Maple leaves danced to the shore-bound breezes
Flashing jade with each fanning that moved them
As they sang green notes to the unsung sea.
Waves crested, hurling spray beyond treetops
Twisting leafy backs to sudden storm winds.
Daydreams ramped up winks in sage
As freshly minted drafts
Flagged their treasured banners.
The sky's bright gusto was a breeze for the wind
As it back-handed palmate maples
Loudly rustling rafts of sails.
Cloud-ships smuggled the storm-snaggled sun
Pirating light, but some bluster still beamed
As tree limbs limbered in sweeping arcs
Pulsing shadows in the grass.
Verdant branches still clung to what kindled
As if they knew that their leaves would have to go
After fall's fired frost blazed them into beauties —
As if they knew that once their colors peaked
They would take their leave —
Stripped like rainbows raked from the wild sky
As if some late day sun-shower
Packed up its prism and left.
But I was just saying it was still spring,
So the maples waved their emerald hands
And they shone and shone and shone.

INTERRUPTED COMMUTE

Last night, beggars bunked under bridges
And everywhere else graffiti bloomed.
They'd tucked themselves in like birds
Under the overpass, their pride
Canvassed under poorly tented nests.
Their bellies roiled
As they mounted the uncertain street
The next morning
When the red light stopped me.
I glimpsed them from my cornered eye:

Panhandlers flagging me down with cardboard pleas,
Trafficking threats to my bubbled journey.
I told myself they must all be addicts
And wondered if hell was a place
Or a state of mind.
But my stalled eyes were safe
Behind my windshield
And rolled-up windows.
Then the endless light changed.

Inside, part of me swallowed a cheer.
I hated to admit it.
I pulled away from my reflection in their eyes
Glad I had to get to work.

THE FISHING TRIP

The waves came up on shore, speaking in tongues
While I waited for the ocean's pitched language
To match the tenor of my heart
So I could understand it.
My sea rubbed salt in its wounds over and over
While I looked at my feet and shored up nothing.
My self-proclaimed genius
Whined with a swollen head — its surf
Unable to quiet itself.

I floated comfortably on catastrophe,
Drifting with self-pity as I worshiped past shipwrecks
Blaming the weather for my storms.
The full moon could not light the darkness
Of my pill-filled room.
But I was going to tell you how my son
Became a man when I wasn't looking
And how I'd lost him at every sunset for years —

About how he left the house to escape
With his better life, and how my marrow knew
How he sheltered me for so long
As he tried to help me right down to his bones.
He had to leave my weakness night after night
As he outgrew me while I sat alone
Trolling the smoky basement of my victim house.
Much later, I told him I was sorry
For a lot of things.

He was much better with it than I was.
He'd already grown up with my totterings.
He'd already felt the death of a good friend.
Then my son taught me how to fish for fun
And cast my lines until I didn't care
How many times my hook got caught in the weeds
Or how many times my worm got stolen.

DIVORCE RECORD - 1970

Years ago, records made their opus sing
And played love's songbook
Ring by ring. Raised circles on the vinyl
Went 'round and 'round
Steering the smitten stylus
Until gaps between ballads blindly silenced notes
Unlinking their heart's chamber music.

Once, they were able to slip out of their clothes
Like albums gently eased from clinging sleeves
And they handled love reverently as bone china.
But their music became flawed with disharmony
With the chipped diamond and scratched record
Each blaming the other for building static
With every passage they scraped over.

It was the same old ruined record
Rumbling on the turntable
As they tried to turn the tables
On each other. They crooned their tunes
In dissonant keys, with classical themes
About scales of justice
But their chosen background of Bach and Vivaldi
Was not from the romantic period.

They listened with their own dynamics
In measured, clever language,
Scoring each other in counterpoint,
So it really didn't matter
How I sat there, afraid to speak
With my frightened child knowing too much
While discord needled deeper into injured places
And too many scars forced the strains of love
To skip away
Becoming too damaged to make music

Turn by turn.

LETHAL INJECTION

It didn't matter where you stood —
It was the way they botched his killing
That got under your skin.
They tried to do it cleanly
But couldn't find the right vein.
People watched the nameless
Trying to get closure with a trinity of drugs
Sewn with revenge needles.
But when things went bad
The curtains closed so no one could see
How the robe of justice unstitched
And clothed its sentence in tatters.

They were only trying to do their job.
Some said he got what he deserved —
Others disagreed. Some weren't sure how to feel.
The victim's family didn't want to talk about it
But reporters called them up anyway
Because the public had the right to know
And the news folks were only doing their job.
The person who answered hung up on them
Leaving them with an empty line
Struggling against restraint
Because they were only trying to live their life
Missing a loved one.

MR. GALLO AT EIGHTY-SEVEN

It wasn't as if I'd been ready
When he told me about his twin dead sons —
About how he and his wife had lost everything
In an eye-blink. We stood in his basement
Beside the two identical new boilers
Standing right next to each other.
I measured the oil in his tanks
While he slowly sized me up.
That's when he told me about his boys —
About how good they'd been —
About how one had gone to Brown
And the other to Boston College.
He'd worked in the cafeteria at Brown
To pay for one son's meal ticket
Sacrificing down to his thin Italian bones
For the other. They were good boys
Both on pre-med scholarships.
He looked at me for a second
And then told me about the accident —
About how they died at the same time —
Too early.
Standing in silence on the dirt floor
I watched him cry
From the deepest place in his house.
Then we went upstairs.
He showed me their pictures
Housed in a double frame.
His wife came home with a bag of groceries

Rescued him without words
And re-told me the story.
She said it had happened 22 years ago —
About as close as yesterday.
I said their life together
Meant something. I showed them
Pictures of my children.
I left them very slowly,
Hearing the boilers start up — the twin fires
Side by side, in their hearts burning.

ON A DAY LIKE THIS

On a day like this, let every star struck night
Pack up its imagination as waking eyes yield
To dawn's burning blooms.
Let daylight delight itself
In tipsy breeze, as gloried sunrise fades
The fabled firmament.
Step out with an expectant spring's light heart
Watching birds flock to seed their wishing sky.
Describe your surprise
At how much the daylight's full moon
Can still move you when it suddens
Into view - as if only
A midnight lover's lamp could inflame passion.

On a day like this, if you walk slowly enough
You might almost forget how yesterday's clouds
Seemed to stunt the world in its reachings
And shadowed your garden with regrets.
You could almost forget
How your blossoms wilted under the starving sun
And how last night's storied points of light emerged
Like so many chaptered heroes
As you farmed your barren sky.

On a day like this, if you start to see how the sun
Can un-clench things, and you hear how every sad
Yesterday song can re-voice itself for another try
It can suddenly seem very important
That you keep walking, and that you watch how birds
Can fly careless and easy in high winds
Or see how the buffeting can help flowers
Shake off rain. You might even see
Lightning-scorched trees and how what's left
Of parts they wouldn't let go of still reach
For the forgiven sky. So choose to walk
And walk some more
And walk as slowly as any new thing
That needs to green in you.

BEACON

We were skipping stones
Across the taut skin of the lake
All afternoon.
But when the span of darkness
Spread its wings
Like crows about to perch
The sun shrank away from the world
And plowed its wake under water.
Somewhere a train was receding
From rails below clouds of crimson.
A moving heart stained the ribs
It had just pressed warm.
Between the heavy seconds, sleep
Tugged our eyes, and dreams
Rippled out from an endlessly drowning ship —
The beacon gone
Over the lid of the lake.

SPRING DECISION

After each long winter
Spring needs to be reborn
To keep us in the world.

Even the coldest things
Have to bow to its greening gift.
You might discover
The smell of some wonderful thaw

That doesn't know
When you've said too much
Or not enough.

Look, the flowers are so many
They can't be named.

Buds peek up to their second lives
Sprinkling edges of winter's withdrawal

With spring in their rooting step
Knowing nothing at all
Except to let themselves be pulled
Towards light.